Wheels
All Around

by Anne Lawrence
photos by Ken O'Donoghue

 HOUGHTON MIFFLIN   BOSTON

Wheels, wheels, all around,
roll and spin all over town.

Little wheels roll out to play.
Big wheels roll to work all day.

Cars and tractors, trucks and trikes,
motor homes and motorbikes –

Wheels, wheels, all around,
roll and spin all over town.

Planes go rolling, then they fly.
Trains go rolling – wave good-bye!

Wheels can roll from here to there.
Wheels go rolling everywhere.

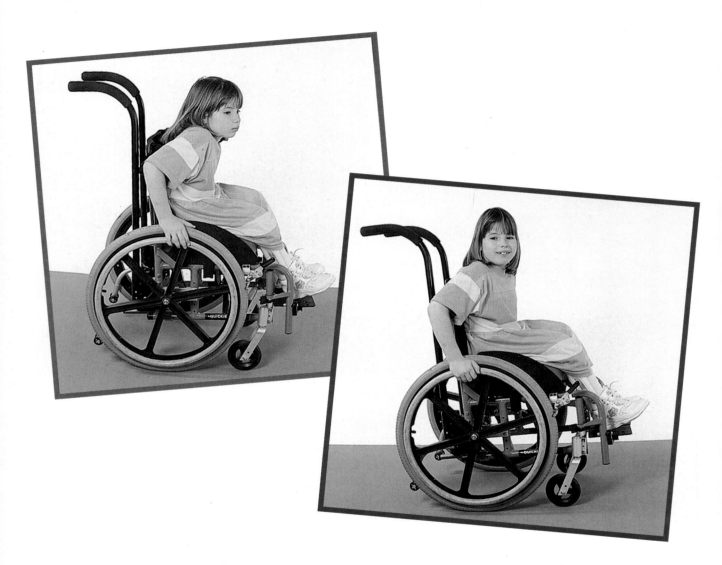

Wheels are used on special chairs.
Wheels are at the county fair.

Wheels go spinning, round and round,
One side up, and one side down.

Push!

The wheels will help it go.

Pull!
The wheels go fast or slow.

Wagons, planes, trucks and cars,
See how many wheels there are!